WATER

Christopher McHugh

Wayland

Discovering art

Animals
Faces
Food
People at Work
Town and Country
Water

Cover The Pool of London, *a scene of the River Thames painted by André Derain. The Tate Gallery, London.*

Editor: Rosemary Ashley
Designer: David Armitage

First published in 1992 by
Wayland (Publishers) Limited
61 Western Road, Hove
East Sussex BN3 1JD
England

British Library Cataloguing in Publication Data
McHugh, Christopher
   Water. – (Discovering Art Series)
   I. Title.   II. Series
   704.9

   ISBN 0–7502–0464–8

Typset by Type Study, Scarborough, England
Printed in Italy by G. Canale & C.S.p.A., Turin
Bound in Belgium by Casterman S.A.

Contents

1 Showing water in art

This book is about water and about art. People have always made many kinds of pictures and objects which we call art. This book will show you some of them. It will show you how people have shown water in their art in different places and at different times.

Water, of course, is very important to people; without it they cannot live. They need it for drinking and cooking, and for the growth of the plants and animals that they use as food. People also use water in other ways; for washing, travelling, carrying things, making things work (the first factories used running water from rivers to drive the machinery).

1 In the well of the great wave of Kanagawa *by the famous Japanese artist Katsushika Hokusai. Reproduced by courtesy of Christies, London.*

2 Niagara Falls *painted by the American artist Frederick Edwin Church. National Gallery of Scotland.*

Water is important to people for all sorts of reasons. Some people have lived by catching fish from it. Others have depended on rain and rivers to make their crops and animals grow. Ships have sailed along rivers and across the sea, carrying goods to sell to others. Some ships have carried armies to conquer other lands.

Often people have built villages or cities on the banks of rivers or at the edges of seas. They have even lived on top of the water itself. Different ways of living have needed different kinds of art; pictures to hang on walls, decorated pots to hold liquid, gardens in which to relax . . .

Pictures **1** and **2** on these pages show the natural power and beauty of water in very different styles. Can you see the rainbow in picture **2**? Rainbows can sometimes be seen when sun shines through tiny drops of water in the air.

2 Water in ancient art

We need water to survive. So did people who lived thousands of years ago. Many have shown water in their art. Here are pictures from three of the oldest civilizations.

In Ancient Egypt most people lived close to the River Nile. Some rich Egyptians had beautiful gardens. Water was taken from the River Nile to help the gardens grow. Picture **3** shows a garden with a pond in it. Look at the way the trees around the pond have been painted. This painting, on the wall of a tomb, shows how important water was to the Egyptians.

3 *A wall painting of a garden with an ornamental pond, from the tomb of Nebamun, Thebes.*

The Ancient Greeks were skilful sailors. They built fast ships and sailed all around the Mediterranean Sea. You can see a ship in picture **4**. It is painted on the side of a vase. The picture tells the story of the hero Odysseus, who is returning home after his adventures. The winged creatures above the ship are called sirens. Their beautiful singing was believed to charm sailors and lead them to their death. Many Greek myths are about the sea.

4 Odysseus and the sirens. *A decorated vase in the British Museum, London.*

The Romans travelled on the sea too. Picture **5** is a mosaic showing two Romans in a fishing boat, with fish and a dolphin.

These three pictures show art made to decorate special places or objects; a wall, a vase and a floor. A picture painted straight on to a wall is called a mural (picture **3**). Pictures or patterns on pottery are usually called decoration (picture **4**). The Roman picture (**5**) is a mosaic, which is a picture made by glueing tiny pieces of stone or glass into the floor or wall.

Did you notice how all of these pictures use strong, clear outlines to show the figures and backgrounds?

5 Fishermen in a boat. *A mosaic from Utica, North Africa. Now in the British Museum, London.*

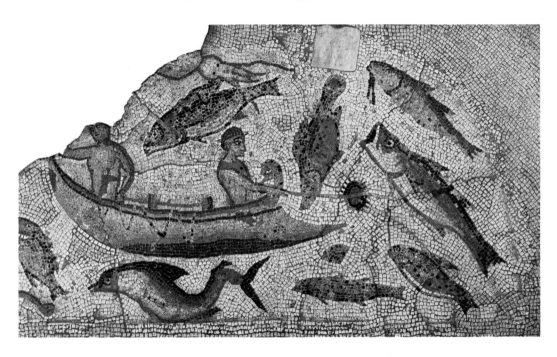

3 Water around the world

The pictures here show some of the different arts from around the world. China and India are very large countries with many millions of people living in them. They are two of the oldest and most important countries of Asia.

It often helps to look at works of art to find out what has happened in earlier times. Sometimes, looking at the way a work of art is made can explain events in history. Picture **6** (opposite) shows a small painting, called a miniature, made in India around 1590. It is very like the miniatures made about the same time in nearby Persia (today called Iran). This gives a clue as to what had happened. Persians had invaded parts of India and set up the Mogul Empire. They brought with them their ideas on how to make pictures.

Picture **7** shows a beautiful garden in a palace at the Alhambra, in Granada, Spain. The garden was laid out by the Moors. They were an Islamic people who ruled Spain for hundreds of years. The palaces of the Alhambra still show the Moorish influence, especially in the wonderful use of water in courtyards and gardens.

7 Water gardens laid out by the Moors at the Palace of Alhambra, Granada, Spain.

The Chinese picture of water, picture **8**, comes from the decoration on a plate. The swirling lines beautifully describe the movement of the waves. Can you see how this picture is like the print called *The Wave*, picture **1**, on page 4? Japanese artists were very influenced by Chinese artists, especially in their use of curving lines.

8 *A Chinese Dragon dish produced during the reign of Yung Cheng, c. 1730.*

6 *An Indian miniature showing two princes, titled* Munim Khan and Khan Zamen in a boat on the river Ganga. *Victoria and Albert Museum, London.*

4 Water in European art

Following the end of the Roman Empire there was a period of change and violence in Europe. We now call this period the Dark Ages.

At this time many peoples were entering Europe from the east and the north, forcing those already there to move further west and south. Much of European life remained unsettled for several hundred years.

The Bayeux Tapestry, picture **9**, is a famous work of art which shows these violent times of change. Made after the Battle of Hastings (in 1066), it shows the story of the Norman invasion of England. This was the beginning of a long period when the histories and the arts of England and France were very closely linked. Often the two countries shared the same king.

9 *A detail from the Bayeux Tapestry, Musée de Bayeux, France.*

10 *(opposite) A painting showing the Christian fleet attacking a port during the Crusades.*

Gradually the Christian Church started to play a part in sorting out the confusion in Europe. The Crusades began and Christians went off to fight the peoples of Islam. Picture **10** shows the crusading knights setting sail for the Holy Land, to try to capture it from the Muslims. Picture **11** is part of a stained glass window from a church in France. It shows the Bible story of Jonah who escaped from the belly of a whale. The thick black lines are strips of lead which hold the pieces of coloured glass in place. Inside the church the sun shines through the glass, making the colours light up and the outlines seem even darker.

After the Middle Ages came the period called the Renaissance. This was the time when people remembered the ideas of Ancient Greece and Rome.

11 *A stained glass window in a church at Mulhouse, France showing the Bible story of Jonah escaping from the whale.*

In picture **12**, Piero della Francesca shows the Bible story of Christ being baptized with water from the River Jordan. How would you describe the difference in the way the water is shown in this picture and in the stained glass window (picture **11**)?

The Renaissance began a process of change during which the Christian Church became less powerful. Artists began to make pictures which had no religious subject. Claude Lorraine, in picture **13**, has painted a religious subject, but the view of sea, city and sky was his real interest.

By Claude's time artists had become more skilful at painting pictures that showed solid objects and the space around them. They did this by showing light and shadow clearly, and by not using strong outlines. Can you see where Piero and Claude have done this in their pictures **12** and **13** on this page?

12 The Baptism of Christ *by Piero della Francesco, reproduced by courtesy of the Trustees, The National Gallery, London.*

12

13 *(left)* Seaport with the Embarkation of Saint Ursula, *by Claude Lorraine.*

14 *(above)* A Lady and Gentleman taking coffee with children in a garden *by Nicolas Lancret. Both paintings reproduced by courtesy of The National Gallery, London.*

In picture **14** the artist has painted a garden scene showing rich people enjoying themselves. The water appears only as a small fountain, there to make the garden prettier. The family are relaxing in the garden, having a cup of chocolate served to them. This French picture was painted in a style called Rococo. At this time things designed for the rich (especially furniture and ornaments) were meant to be pretty, delicate and amusing. Soon after, the poor people of France rebelled against their king in what became known as the French Revolution.

5 Seafarers

15 Four Day's Fight by Abraham Storck, is a painting of a sea battle between the Dutch and the English. The National Maritime Museum, London.

Trade became more important in Europe during the Middle Ages and the Renaissance. Ships were used for trade, and to carry soldiers for conquest of other lands. The Spanish, for example, grew rich because of gold they brought back from the Americas. In the 1500s, Spain also ruled the Netherlands, but after years of struggle, people from the northern region broke free to become the Independent Dutch Republic.

At this time there was an upheaval in the Christian Church. This was called the Protestant Reformation. The Reformation meant that people could follow other (Protestant) branches of the Christian religion, so the Catholic Church grew much less powerful. Rich people built houses rather than palaces, and bought paintings to hang in them. Everyday subjects became popular, showing things that were familiar to the Dutch people: the countryside (landscape), objects on tables (still life), people (portraits), everyday activities (genre) and boats and the sea (marine or seascape).

Boats and the sea were very important to the Dutch because much of their country was coastline. Sea trade was vital to their lives.

Picture **15** is a beautiful example of Dutch marine painting from the 1600s. It shows the skills of a Dutch artist, who painted the sea and ships in realistic detail. The painting tells the dramatic story of a sea battle between the Dutch and English. The battle, which took place in the English Channel, lasted for four days and, although the English won, they lost a great many men and ships.

16 A Winter Scene with Skaters near a Castle *by Hendrik Avercamp, reproduced by courtesy of the Trustees, The National Gallery, London.*

Picture **16** is a Dutch genre painting, showing people enjoying fun and games on water frozen over with ice in the winter.

The English, like the Dutch, were becoming important sea traders. Their painters, too, liked to paint scenes of ships and the sea. Landscape paintings were also becoming popular in Britain. The painting below (**17**), by Joseph Wright, is an unusual painting of an Italian

17 *Joseph Wright of Derby (the name he is always known by) painted this picture lit by moonlight. He called it* A Moonlight with a Lighthouse. *The Tate Gallery, London.*

landscape at night. The moonlight gives a mysterious feeling and the artist uses very dark colours, which make the reflections on the water all the more interesting.

Being surrounded by sea, Britain depended on ships and the navy for its success in trade and the building of an empire. So it is not surprising that paintings of shipping and the sea became popular. Joseph Mallord William Turner is often said to be England's greatest painter, and, as we can see from pictures **18** and **19**, he was very interested in marine subjects. Turner was born and grew up in London, near to the River Thames. All through his childhood he watched the ships coming and going and the effects of sunlight and weather on the river. As he grew older, Turner became more and more fascinated by the effects of light.

18 The Fighting Temeraire *by Joseph Mallord William Turner, reproduced by courtesy of the Trustees, The National Gallery, London.*

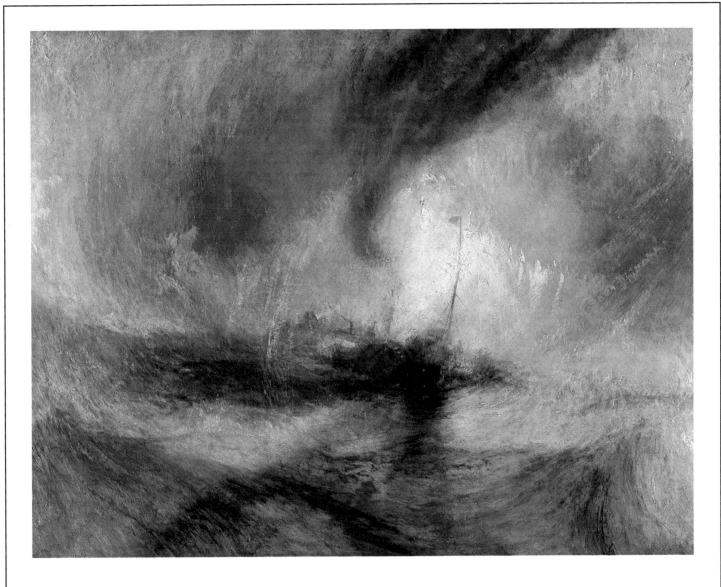

The Fighting Temeraire (picture **18**) is a famous painting putting together ships, sunlight and sea. What colours has Turner used to show sunlight in this painting?

Snowstorm (picture **19**) was painted after Turner had travelled through a terrible storm on a steam ferry. He asked the sailors to tie him to the mast so that he could see and feel the storm directly, without being washed overboard! Do you think the painting describes the sea storm well?

These pictures were made with oil paint. This is usually painted on to wood, or cloth called canvas which is held tight and flat by being pinned on to a frame. Oil paint can be used in thin or thick layers. It can make layers that can be seen through but which alter the colours beneath.

19 Snowstorm. Steamboat off a Harbour Mouth *by Joseph Mallord William Turner. This painting is in the Turner Collection at the Tate Gallery, London, where a large number of his paintings can be seen together.*

6 Light on the water

Turner and another English painter, John Constable, were two artists who influenced French painters of landscape in the 1800s. The most famous of these painters are called the Impressionists. This was a name given to a group of young artists as a joke, and was meant to suggest that they could not paint properly! The artists in the group were all very different from one another. Some, as the pictures on these pages show, liked painting people. Others preferred to paint landscape pictures, as you can see on the following pages.

Picture **20**, shows two friends in a rowing boat on a lake. It was painted by Berthe Morisot. She often painted pictures of friends, servants and children, in the house or the garden. This was one of the unusual things about the

20 Summer's Day *by Berthe Morisot, reproduced by courtesy of the Trustees, The National Gallery, London.*

21 *A print showing a woman bathing, by the American artist Mary Cassatt.*

Impressionists; they often painted 'ordinary' subjects. Look at how Morisot has painted the water in this picture. How would you describe the difference between her way of painting water and the water shown in picture **3**, page 6?

Mary Cassatt's print, picture **21**, also shows an everyday scene. Do you think this picture is a little like picture **1** (page 4)? Japanese prints, such as *The Wave*, greatly influenced the Impressionist painters and also later artists.

22 Claude Monet in his Floating Studio. *Edouard Manet's painting of his friend, in the Alte Pinakothek, Munich.*

The painting by Edouard Manet, picture **22**, is of another Impressionist, Claude Monet. He is painting in the little boat he used as a studio on the River Seine, in France. Some Impressionists made their paintings on the spot, in front of the subject they were painting. Earlier artists were more likely to make drawings of their subject and then take these back to their studio. There the drawings would be used to help in the messy, complicated business of making a painting.

Monet always loved to paint the River Seine. He had spent his boyhood in the port of Le Havre, where the river meets the sea. Then he studied painting in Paris, where the river runs through the heart of the city. He spent the end of his life in a house with a large garden only a few kilometres from the Seine, at a place called Giverny, between Paris and the coast.

Monet was fascinated by water, weather and, most of all, light. His life was spent trying to capture in his paintings the way light really looks. We all see things only because light bounces off them into our eyes, allowing our brain to make sense of what we see. The light always has to come from somewhere, usually the sun. At night it is artificial light, or the sun reflecting off the moon, which allows us to see things. With no light we would see absolutely nothing. Monet knew all about this and tried to make his paintings by carefully noticing the exact coloured patches of light that came to his eyes.

If you look closely you can see how Monet has tried to put down these patches of light in paint, just as his eyes saw them. Look how he worked quickly to paint the water in picture **23**; you can see the brushmarks. But when

23 The Railway Bridge at Argenteuil *by Claude Monet, Musée de Louvre, Paris.*

looked at from a distance these marks actually look like light, flickering on the surface of moving water. Next time you look at water (a pond, stream, river, puddle or the sea) notice how the light is reflected from it. See how the colours and patterns change as the weather changes.

During the last part of his life, Monet mostly painted subjects in his beautiful garden at Giverny. Often, he returned to paint the water lilies in the pond, which he had specially designed. Picture **24** is one of these paintings, with its dreamy world of reflections. We can see through the surface into the water; we can see the sky reflected from above; and we can see the lilies themselves at the surface, where the sky meets the water.

24 Nympheas, *one of a large group of paintings by Claude Monet, of his lily pond at Giverny. Private collection.*

Picture **25** is an example of a method of painting called Pointilism. This picture is made up of tiny dots or 'points'. Seurat, the inventor of this method, called it Divisionism because in it he divided each colour into dots of the colours which make it up. If he wanted orange, for instance, he would put dots of red and yellow next to each other. At a distance the 'divided' colours join together again and appear to be orange. Seurat got his ideas for this method from the Impressionists – look at the paintings by Monet and see if you can see why. Seurat is one of the artists called a Post-Impressionist, because he came just after the Impressionists. Printing works in a similar way to Pointilism. Have a close look at a poster and see if you can see the coloured dots.

25 Le Bec du Hoc, Grandcamp, *a sea cliff in Normandy painted by Georges Seurat. The Tate Gallery, London.*

7 Art in the twentieth century

It is not easy to show water in art, though this book has shown you several ways in which artists have gone about it. Water is clear, it has no edges, and it constantly moves and changes shape.

Picture **2** (page 5) showed a very realistic painting of water, but this type of painting was no longer necessary after the invention of photography in the 1830s. Impressionists found a way of painting showing a sense of movement, but later artists wanted to experiment even more. They used bright colours to show what they felt as well as what they saw.

The most important thing in André Derain's painting of the River Thames, on the cover of this book, is the way he has put strong colours next to each other. They give us a feeling of action and excitement. Raoul Dufy also painted bright, energetic pictures, like this lively harbour scene, picture **26**. Dufy and Derain were members of a group of French painters nicknamed *Les Fauves* (meaning Wild Beasts) because of their bright colours and energetic way of painting.

26 Deauville, Drying the Sails, *a colourful harbour scene by Raoul Dufy. The Tate Gallery, London.* © *DACS 1992.*

27 The Scream, *a famous painting by Edvard Munch. National Gallery, Oslo.*

Picture **27**, by Edvard Munch, at the bottom of the opposite page, was made at the end of the 1800s. In this picture the artist is trying to show his feelings. The colours and lines make water, bridge, land and sky seem to become part of the scream uttered by the skeleton-like person in the foreground.

John Sloan was a member of a group of artists working in New York called the 'Ashcan School'. They were called this because they liked to paint everyday, even ugly or dirty, city subjects. Sloan's picture, **28**, shows a view from the back of a ferry-boat between islands in New York Harbour. He has made the air look thick with dampness and the deck shiny with water.

28 The Wake of the Ferry II *by John Sloan, The Phillips Collection, Washington DC.*

29 They're Biting *by Paul Klee, The Tate Gallery, London.*

Earlier in this book we have seen how, after the Middle Ages, artists began to draw and paint with softer outlines. They used light and shade, rather than strong lines in their pictures. Impressionist painters often used no outlines at all.

Nowadays, artists do not have to paint pictures showing things as they really are: photography, films and videos can do that. So they are free to make any kind of art they like, using all sorts of materials. They have often borrowed ideas and ways of making art from earlier times, including using strong outlines.

Paul Klee's painting, picture **29** (opposite) is an imagined world, where strange creatures wait to catch strange fish. Everything can be seen at once, above and below water; and everything is described by a line. What can you see in this picture?

Arshile Gorky was an American artist who was born in Armenia, in Asia. He painted *Waterfall* (picture **30**). It is not meant to be a picture of a real waterfall but perhaps a picture about movement which is like the movement of falling water. Paintings like this mean that we must do some work. We have to decide what meaning the shapes and the colours may have. What do you think about this picture? Look at it for a while and try to decide if it makes you feel or think anything . . .

Picture **31** shows water with bright colours and shapes. When you go to a swimming pool, look for the patterns of light on the water. Think how you would show them.

30 The Waterfall *by Arshile Gorky, The Tate Gallery, London.* © *ADAGP, Paris and DACS, London 1992.*

31 Afternoon Swimming *by David Hockney, reproduced by courtesy of Christies, London.* © *D. Hockney 1979.*

Who are the artists and where are their works?

Hendrik Avercamp (1585–1634) Dutch
A painter of landscape and genre pictures who specialized in winter scenes. His paintings can be seen in the Netherlands, the USA, and in Edinburgh and London. Picture **16**, page 15.

Mary Cassatt (1845–1926) American
An Impressionist painter whose favourite subjects were mothers and children. She worked in Paris, and was greatly influenced by Japanese prints. Her work can be seen mainly in the USA. Picture **21**, page 19.

Frederick Edwin Church (1826–1900) American
A painter of huge, dramatic landscapes. He was one of a group of artists known as the Hudson River school and his work can be seen mainly in various American collections. Picture **2**, page 5.

Claude Lorraine (real name Claude Gellée) (1600–82) French
He was greatly influenced by his travels and study in Italy. His paintings looking into setting suns were a direct influence on Turner and other artists. His work can be seen in important collections around the world. Picture **13**, page 12.

André Derain (1880–1954) French
One of the Fauves (Wild Beasts). He painted with very bright colours and energetic technique. His paintings can be seen in France, and in major collections throughout the world, including the Tate Gallery, London. **Cover**.

Raoul Dufy (1877–1953) French
Also a member of the Fauve group. In later life he painted scenes of enjoyment in bright colours – horse races, seaside towns etc – and made designs for cloth and pottery. There are large collections of his work in France, in New York and at the Tate Gallery and Courtauld Institute in London. Picture **26**, page 24.

Arshile Gorky (1904–48) Armenian/American
He left Armenia for the USA as a teenager. He was an important link between European art and a new American style known as Abstract Expressionism. His works can be seen in various collections, especially in the USA. Picture **31**, page 27.

David Hockney (b 1937) English
A painter who became famous in the 1960s, during the period of Pop Art (a style based on the use of familiar objects in unusual ways). He lives and works mainly in the USA. He is also famous for his stage designs, especially for operas. His work can be seen in Bradford and at the Tate Gallery in London, and in collections throughout the world. Picture **31**, page 27.

Katsushika Hokusai (1760–1849) Japanese
One of the most famous artists of the *Ukiyo-e* style of painting. His work can be seen at the Fitzwilliam Museum, Cambridge, the British Museum, Victoria and Albert Museum, London, and in museums and galleries throughout the world. Picture **1**, page 4.

Paul Klee (1879–1940) Swiss/German
A printer and painter who studied and worked in Switzerland and Germany. His travels in North Africa influenced his feeling for colour. He was connected to the 'Blue Rider' and 'The Blue Four' – famous groups of artists in Germany. His works are in major collections throughout the world but especially at Berne, Switzerland. Picture **29**, page 26.

Nicolas Lancret (1690–1743) French
A painter of the Rococo period, usually painting pictures of groups of people in gardens. He was greatly influenced by the famous Rococo artist, Jean Antoine Watteau. His works can be seen in the Wallace Collection in London, and in Paris. Picture **14**, page 13.

Edouard Manet (1832–83) French
After studying Spanish paintings he developed a style using a lot of black and white, which he later changed for a softer, Impressionist style, and leaving black out altogether. Two of his most famous pictures (*Le Déjeuner Sur L'Herbe* and *Olympia*) were thought shocking when they were first exhibited in Paris. His paintings can be seen in famous collections throughout the world. Picture **22**, page 20.

Claude Monet (1840–1926) French
The leading Impressionist painter. See pages 20–22. His painting *Impression; sunrise*, which was first shown in 1874, gave the name to the Impressionist movement. Monet's works can be seen in galleries throughout the world, and especially in Musées Marmottan, d'Orsay and de l'Orangerie in Paris, France. Pictures **23** and **24**, pages 21 and 22.

Berthe Morisot (1841–95) French
She was an Impressionist painter who often painted 'domestic' scenes with great tenderness and skill. Morisot was important also in helping others in the Impressionist group to keep working, and in organizing sales and exhibitions. Her works can be seen in Boston and Washington (USA), Paris (France) and the National and Tate Galleries in London. Picture **20**, page 18.

Edvard Munch (1863–1944) Norwegian
A painter who spent much time in France and Germany. He painted pictures about life, death, love and feelings. He was an important influence on a group of young German artists called the Expressionists. His works can be seen in major collections around the world, including Oslo (Norway) and the Tate Gallery in London. Picture **27**, page 24.

Piero della Francesca (c1410–1492) Italian
A painter of the Renaissance. His pictures have great stillness and calm. Many of Piero's most important works were painted on to the walls of churches in a technique called fresco. His works can be seen in various towns in Italy, in USA, and in London and Oxford. Picture **12**, page 12.

Georges Seurat (1859–1891) French
He invented Pointilism after studying the methods of the Impressionists and he also studied scientific theories of colour (see page 23). His paintings can be seen in important galleries around the world and in London, Edinburgh, Glasgow and Liverpool. Picture **25**, page 23.

John Sloan (1871–1951) American
He worked as a journalist–artist, making drawings for newspapers in Philadelphia and New York. He was a member of the Ashcan school, so-called because of their interest in everyday and even ugly subjects. His paintings can be seen in Washington, New York, Philadelphia and other US cities. Picture **28**, page 25.

Abraham Storck (1644–c1708) Dutch
The youngest and best known of three brothers born and based in Amsterdam. He specialized in pictures of boating festivals, but also painted sea battles and occasionally town views. His works can be seen in galleries, mainly in the Netherlands. Picture **15**, p. 14.

Joseph Mallord William Turner (1775–1851) English
A painter especially of the sea and landscape. He painted thousands of pictures in both oil paint and watercolour. The largest collection of Turner's works are in the Clore Gallery at the Tate, London. Pictures **18** and **19**, pages 16 and 17.

Joseph Wright of Derby (1734–97) English
A painter of portraits and of genre scenes showing scientific experiments and people in landscapes. He was famous for painting the new successful men of industry in and around Derby, England. His works can be seen at Derby and in the Tate Gallery, London. Picture **17**, page 15.

Glossary

Ashcan school A group of American painters who worked in New York at the end of the 19th and early 20th centuries. Noted for their paintings of everyday subjects.

Brushmark The mark left by a brush in painting.

Catholic Church The branch of Christianity headed by the Pope.

Christian Someone who practises Christianity, the religion based on the teachings of Jesus Christ.

Civilizations Stages in the development of the way people live together in groups.

Crusades Expeditions in the Middle Ages, when Christian soldiers tried to recapture the Holy Land from the Muslims.

Dark Ages A period of violence and confusion in Europe, from the late 5th to 10th centuries AD.

Empire A group of countries governed by one ruler.

Figure In pictures this usually means a person or a body.

Foreground The nearest part of a scene or picture.

Fresco A way of painting straight on to newly plastered walls.

Genre Describing a picture of people doing everyday activities.

Islamic To do with Islam, the religion that follows the teachings of the Prophet Muhammed. Islamic people are called Muslims.

Landscape A picture of the countryside, sometimes including buildings.

Middle Ages The period between the end of the Dark Ages and the Renaissance, from the 6th to 16th centuries AD.

Miniatures Very small paintings.

Moors An Islamic people from north-west Africa.

Mogul Empire The Muslim Empire that ruled large parts of India, from the 16th to 18th centuries.

Myths Stories about heroes and gods of ancient times.

Norman Relating to Normandy in northern France. The Normans invaded and conquered Britain in 1066.

Oil paint A type of paint in which the colour is held together with linseed or poppy seed oil.

Pointilism A method of painting using dots of colour (sometimes called Divisionism).

Portrait A picture of a person intended to be a record of what that person looks like.

Protestant religion Any of the Churches that separated from the Catholic Church to follow the principles of the Reformation.

Realistic Having a believable appearance.

Reformation The religious movement of the 16th century which resulted in the establishment of Protestant Churches.

Renaissance A time of rediscovery in Europe of ideas from Classical Greece and Rome, which occurred in the 16th century.

Rococo A light, delicate style of painting and design, mainly in 18th-century France.

Seascape A picture of the sea (also called marine).

Still life A picture of objects indoors, usually on a table of some kind.

Tapestry A decorative hanging for walls, made by weaving a picture or design into the material.

Watercolour A painting made with watercolour paints, which are mixed with water and applied in thin washes of colour.

Books to read

The Book of Art – A Way of Seeing (Ernest Benn, 1979).

Every Picture Tells a Story by Rolf Harris (Phaidon, 1989).

Great Painters by Piero Ventura (Kingfisher, 1989).

Just Look . . . A Book about Paintings by Robert Cumming (Viking Kestrel, 1986).

Painting and Sculpture by Jillian Powell (Wayland, 1989).

Penguin Dictionary of Art and Artists by Peter and Linda Murray (Penguin, 1989).

20th Century Art by Jillian Powell (Wayland, 1989).

Water – through the eyes of artists by Wendy and Jack Richardson (Macmillan, 1990).

Index

Picture acknowledgements

The publishers have attempted to contact all copyright holders of the illustrations in this title, and apologise if there have been any oversights.

The photographs in this book were supplied by: Bridgeman Art Library 4, 16, 18, 20, 21, 22, 27(lower); Sonia Halliday 11(top); Michael Holford 6, 7(both), 9(lower), 10; National Gallery 12, 13(both), 15(top), 18; National Gallery of Scotland 5; Phillips Collection 25; Ronald Sheridan Library 9(top); Tony Stone Worldwide 8; Tate Gallery cover, 15(lower), 17, 23, 24(top), 26, 27(top).

The following paintings appear by kind permission of the copyright holders; *Pool of London* by André Derain on the cover © ADAGP, Paris and DACS, London 1992; *Sails Drying at Deauville* by Raoul Dufy, page 24 © DACS 1992; *Waterfall* by Arshile Gorky, page 27 © ADAGP, Paris and DACS, London 1992; and *Afternoon Swimming* © D. Hockney 1979 page 27.